THE KOREAN WAR

THE KOREAN WAR

Carter Smith

Silver Burdett Press, Inc.
Englewood Cliffs, New Jersey

Acknowledgments

The author thanks the following individuals and institutions for their invaluable help in text and picture research: Mr. Nat Andriani, Wide World Photos; Mr. John Barnett, the U.S. Navy Art Center; Lt. Colonel Mark H. Coon, the U.S. Military Monuments Commission; the Department of the Army, Chief of Military History; Mrs. Sook Kih Park, the Korea Overseas Information Service; Mr. Thomas Prendergast, Chief of the United Nations Photo Unit; Mr. Bernard Reilly, the Library of Congress; the Staff of the National Archives; Mr. Martin M. Teasley, the Dwight D. Eisenhower Library; and Mr. Benedict K. Zobrist, the Harry S. Truman Library.

Consultants

We thank the following people for reviewing the manuscript and offering their helpful suggestions:

Hung Woong Pak
Writer and Educational Consultant
Member, Asian Task Force of Philadelphia
    School District
Member, Board of School Directors,
    Cheltenham Township, Pennsylvania

Richard M. Haynes
Assistant Professor
Division of Administration, Curriculum and Instruction
Director of the Office of Field Experiences and Teacher
    Placement, School of Education and Psychology
Western Carolina University

Cover: Navy medical corpsman advancing to help the crews of two Marine tanks caught by North Korean artillery fire. From a watercolor by Hugh Cabot III. Courtesy of the U.S. Navy Art Center.

Title Page: Two U.S. Army 155-millimeter howitzers light up the night sky in front of Seoul in 1950. National Archives.

Contents Page: The United Nations Korean Service Medal. Courtesy of the United Nations.

Back Cover: Detail of painting of the UN forces landing at Inchon on September 15, 1950. From a painting by Herbert C. Hahn. Courtesy of the U.S. Navy Art Center.

Library of Congress Cataloging-in-Publication Data

Smith, Carter.
    The Korean War/Carter Smith.
        p. cm. —(Turning points in American History.)
    Includes bibliographical references.
    Summary: Describes the people, places and events
surrounding the Korean War.
    1. Korean War, 1950-1953—Juvenile literature. [1. Korean War,
1950-1953.] I. Title.   II. Series: Turning points in American
history.
DS918.S58   1990
951.904'2—dc20
                                                    90-8421
                                                    CIP
                                                    AC

Editorial Coordination by Richard G. Gallin

 Created by Media Projects Incorporated

C. Carter Smith, *Executive Editor*
Toni Rachiele, *Managing Editor*
Charles A. Wills, *Project Editor*
Bernard Schleifer, *Design Consultant*
Arlene Goldberg, *Cartographer*

ISBN 0-382-09953-2 [lib. bdg.]
10 9 8 7 6 5 4 3 2 1

ISBN 0-382-09949-4 [pbk.]
10 9 8 7 6 5 4 3 2 1

CONTENTS

INTRODUCTION

SUDDENLY, "A HUMAN SEA OF CHINESE INFANTRY"

On Friday morning, November 24, 1950, General Douglas MacArthur, Supreme Commander of the United Nations (UN) Forces in Korea, made an announcement at his Tokyo headquarters. The general reported that his forces had launched a major offensive in Korea in an effort to end the brief but bloody war his UN forces had been fighting. The UN's goal in this "police action" was to eject the Communist North Korean invaders from the Republic of Korea (South Korea).

MacArthur's forces had advanced in subfreezing temperatures to the northernmost border—the Yalu River—separating North Korea from Manchuria, the northeastern part of China.

Earlier in the month, the *Korea Times*, an English-language newspaper in Seoul, had described life in the liberated

capital as "returning to normal." The Republic of Korea (ROK) Army headquarters reported, "Our army is continuing its exterminating drive against the enemy, who are taking refuge in the mountains." More than 135,000 Communist prisoners of war were reported to be in UN POW (prisoner of war) camps. North Korean casualties were estimated at more than 330,000. The weary U.S. troops and their families were hearing about the possibility of having "the troops home by Christmas."

This was not to be.

On November 26, more than 300,000 Chinese soldiers swept down on the UN forces across the entire 300-mile width of the Korean peninsula. Using human-wave tactics, they came on night and day, with wild screaming, cymbals, whistles, and scratchy bugles.

The inexperienced Republic of Korea (ROK) troops were overwhelmed almost at once. They fell back in chaos.

U.S. Marines man an observation post atop a barren hill on the Yalu River.

U.S. Army infantrymen advance up the rugged mountains near the Chinese border in November 1950.

The UN forces began a general withdrawal to the south.

U.S. Marine Lieutenant Joseph Owen later wrote of his patrol's discovery of the new enemy:

> We had encountered no enemy since leaving the road more than an hour before. But Kelly, my runner [messenger], insisted, "There are [Chinese] all around us. I can sense them!" he told me, but I saw no sign of them. . . .
>
> "Up there! Look!" Kelly nudged me. A ridgeline 500 yards southwest was crawling with Chinese soldiers looking down at us. . . .
>
> Now we were fully surrounded and the Chinese fire was intense. Several times the enemy charged at our line, but they made no significant penetration. We fought them off, mostly with small arms fire and grenades.

The 25,000 men of the 1st Marine Division were positioned above the Chosin Reservoir on the west central part of the United Nations line. The Republic of Korea Second Corps (a military unit of more than two divisions) on its right had been crushed. A "human sea" of Chinese soldiers was swarming forward all across Korea.

Some units were badly surprised. One marine recalled: "The bugles are the first thing I remember. Then the chaos. There didn't seem to be any sense of order. I was in my sleeping bag, snoozing with my BAR [Browning Automatic Rifle]. A guy who'd been on watch grabbed the bottom of the bag and began dragging me down the hill. He kept hollering, 'They're here! They're here!' A lot of guys must have been caught with their boots off. I saw them running in their stocking feet. It all happened so fast."

Elsewhere in the shock of the attack there were acts of great heroism. Marine Private Hector Cafferata was awarded the Congressional Medal of Honor (America's highest military decoration) for almost single-handedly stopping a Chinese breakthrough. Lieutenant Robert McCarthy described Cafferata's brave action:

> The 3rd Platoon was under extremely heavy attack. The front two squads and the machine gun section of the platoon were overwhelmed by sheer force of numbers. Of the thirty-five Marines in these units, fifteen were killed, nine were wounded, three were missing, and only eight were still effective. . . . Cafferata stood up, com-

This woodcut by Chinese artist Li Hua is captioned "Korean People's Army troops joining forces with Chinese People's Volunteers."

pletely exposing himself to enemy fire, and shot two M1 rifles as fast as a wounded Marine could reload for him. Cafferata also grabbed one Chinese grenade, threw it out of the trench, and pushed two others from the edge of the trench.

Private Cafferata's citation notes that he fought through the night in his stocking feet because he hadn't had time to put on his boots.

There was both chaos and heroism all across the battle line and among the many units of the United Nations Command. Most of the forces under General MacArthur's command were South Korean or U.S. units, but the "Chinese People's Volunteers" also met brave resistance from British units and a brigade of Turkish soldiers.

In the last days of November 1950, the "police action" that had begun five months earlier seemed about to end in a UN victory. But with the coming of the Chinese, the conflict entered a new and ominous phase.

1

THE HERMIT KINGDOM

The ancient land of Korea has been known as both the Land of the Morning Calm and the Hermit Kingdom. Both names are somewhat inaccurate, for the country's history has been anything but calm. While Korea was isolated (somewhat "hermitlike") from the world at large, it has been the scene of bloody wars between its three powerful East Asian neighbors—China, Russia, and Japan—for centuries.

The Korean peninsula stretches about 600 miles south from the eastern rim of Asia. The Chinese region of Manchuria and the Siberian region of the Soviet Union border it on the north. To Korea's west across the Yellow Sea is China, and to the east across the Sea of Japan lie the islands of Japan.

The country is a land of rocky hills and mountains, with only 25 percent of

A ceremony at the capitol building in Seoul marks the founding of the Republic of Korea (South Korea) on April 15, 1948.

the land suitable for farming. Korea's total land area is roughly 85,000 square miles, about half the size of California.

On the map, the peninsula is located between the 34th and 43rd parallels, north of the equator. San Francisco and Philadelphia, on roughly the same line of latitude, enjoy moderate weather. Korea's climate, however, is very different from the climate in these cities.

In Korea, winters are very severe. Bitter winds howl down from Siberia. This makes life miserable for anyone in its rugged mountain or hill country.

Summer temperatures can rise to 110 degrees. Moreover, the monsoon, or rainy season, runs from the end of June through August. The monsoon turns the unpaved roads into rivers of mud.

Korean historians write that the peninsula was first settled thousands of years ago by tribes that came from the Altai Mountains in central Asia. These people migrated eastward to Mongolia, Siberia, and Korea.

Scroll painting depicts court scene during Korea's Yi dynasty.

The people of this farming society were governed by three kingdoms. These emerged around the first century before Christ. One of these kingdoms, Silla, unified the Korean peninsula in 676. In 918, Silla was overthrown and the Koroyo dynasty was established. In 1392, the Yi dynasty was inaugurated. It lasted until 1910.

The Yi kings ruled Korea for over six centuries, but they were troubled by frequent invasions and revolts sparked by their Chinese, Russian, and Japanese neighbors.

In the fifteenth and sixteenth centuries, the country was prosperous. It came to accept a close alliance with China, with whom it shared the Buddhist religion and Confucian philosophy. Although China did not consider Korea its colony, Korea was a "little brother" state to China.

But other nations also sought influence and control over the Hermit Kingdom.

In the late fifteenth century and into the next century, Russia, under Czar Ivan IV (Ivan the Terrible), began to expand eastward to Siberia to the Pacific Ocean. Eventually, Russia reached the frontiers of Manchuria and Korea and the Siberian coast opposite the islands of Japan.

The fact that giant Russia was becoming an Asian power worried Japan's rulers. Also, both Russia and Japan realized they needed Korea to dominate China. Korea's neighbors knew the peninsula was an "invasion highway" in and out of the Asian mainland.

The first move was made by Japan in the 1590s, when it twice invaded Korea. But the Japanese withdrew, and Korea managed to remain isolated from the rest of the world, except for China.

In the 1860s, other nations were seeking trade in Asia. French, German, and U.S. naval expeditions all tried to open up Korea (just as the United States, under Commodore Matthew C. Perry, had done in 1853 with Japan). But none of the three nations was successful.

Then, in 1876, the Japanese sent a military expedition to Korea to force a "treaty of friendship and commerce" upon the Korean government. The treaty opened up ports to foreign ships and established diplomatic relations.

The Chinese then advised their humiliated Korean ally to "check the poison [Japanese expansion] with an antidote." They suggested that Korea form a treaty with a distant nation that was not interested in gaining territory on the Asian mainland.

The United States and Korea signed a treaty of friendship and commerce in 1882. Similar trading arrangements had been made with Russia, Great Britain, and all the other major European powers by 1893.

Japan realized that it must move strongly if it was going to have any influence over Korea. Japan's foreign minister stated publicly that Korea "should be made part of the Japanese map." Riots between pro-Chinese and pro-Japanese groups in Korea gave the Japanese the excuse they needed. They

A Korean nobleman of the Yi dynasty.

sent an army to Korea once again. In 1894, war broke out between China and Japan.

The Chinese-Japanese War of 1894–95 was fought mostly over which nation was to control the Korean peninsula and the Yellow Sea. The Japanese army and navy, which had been trained by European officers, overwhelmed the Chinese. The treaty ending the war recognized that Korea was independent of China. This allowed the Japanese to

Japanese cavalry on patrol in Korea in 1904, during the Russo-Japanese War.

dominate Korea without Chinese influence. The Koreans fought against the Japanese domination of their country. They also rejected their traditional relationship with China, turning to Russia for support. In 1896, Korea's King Kojong fled to the Russian Embassy. Russia sent political advisers and established further commercial ventures.

A war broke out again in 1904, this time between Japan and Russia. Japan won decisively in the Russo-Japanese War. The Japanese naval victory in the Strait of Tsushima, a few miles off the Korean port of Pusan, was the final key battle of that war. The Treaty of Portsmouth, arranged in 1905 with the help of U.S. President Theodore Roosevelt, formally acknowledged Japan's authority in Korea.

Japan now had the complete control it had sought over the Korean peninsula. A protectorate arrangement (a protecting military occupation) was maintained until 1910. In that year, the last Korean king was forced out. The

Land of Morning Calm was annexed to become part of "the map of Japan." Japan's centuries-old dream of a bridge from its island homeland to the Asian mainland seemed complete, at the expense of the humiliated Koreans.

For the next thirty-five years, the Japanese maintained a ruthless rule designed to exploit Korea. Many Koreans fought back. There were frequent uprisings, and in 1907 a guerrilla war, which started in the countryside and the mountains, lasted for several years. P. A. McKensie, a foreigner who visited the guerrilla forces in the hills, reported on "the strong hand of Japan. . . . I beheld in front of me village after village reduced to ashes. Destruction, thorough and complete, had fallen upon it. Not a single house was left, and not a single wall of a house."

As the Japanese succeeded in putting down the guerrilla fighters, more and more patriotic Korean leaders fled the country. To stay meant imprisonment, torture, and often execution.

One such leader was Syngman Rhee. Rhee had been jailed by Japan between 1897 and 1904 for protesting Japan's control of Korea. After his release, Rhee went to the United States to enlist American aid for his country. He also attended American universities. He returned to Korea, but was again forced to flee to the United States in 1912. In 1919, Rhee was elected president of a Korean provisional government (an anti-Japanese government-in-exile) with offices in Vladivostok (Russia), Shanghai (China), and Hawaii. The Japanese put

Guerrillas of the Korean Righteous Army fought a brave but futile war against the Japanese occupation in the early twentieth century.

a price on Rhee's head, and he was not to return to his native land until 1945, after the defeat of Japan in World War II.

Rhee worked tirelessly to get the major powers to help his efforts for a free and independent Korea. But his hopes were in vain.

Japan's hunger for land was growing. In 1931, it once again invaded the Chinese region of Manchuria, creating a puppet state it called Manchukuo. The world was in a severe economic depression, and neither China nor Russia could step in to get the Japanese out. Then, in 1937, Japan launched a full-scale attack on China, a war that was to go on for eight years.

Japan's 1941 sneak attack on the U.S. fleet at Pearl Harbor in Hawaii brought the United States into World War II. The Japanese were successful at first, capturing the Philippines and much of China and Southeast Asia. But in the end they were completely defeated, surrendering on August 15, 1945.

With the worldwide conflict ended, the victors gathered to redraw the maps of both Europe and Asia according to the war's results. This "geography of victory" would lead to continued conflict, especially in Korea.

America's major allies in the war in the Pacific were China, Great Britain, along with other British Commonwealth nations, and the Soviet Union (U.S.S.R.), which came into the war in the Pacific less than a month before the surrender.

Syngman Rhee's efforts had influenced the Allies. In a 1943 meeting of the Allied leaders, in Cairo, Egypt, a pledge to create a free and independent Korea "in due course" was included in what was called the Cairo Declaration.

In early August 1945, with the war ending, the Russians had moved swiftly. They sent 100,000 troops into northern Korea. In what was to have been only a temporary arrangement, the Allies agreed that U.S. forces would

Koreans and Chinese residents of Seoul greet the U.S. troops that liberated the city from the Japanese in 1945.

accept the surrender of Japanese troops south of the 38th parallel. The USSR would do so north of the parallel, about 35 miles north of Seoul. At an Allied meeting in Moscow later in 1945, the United States, the Soviet Union, Britain, and China agreed to establish a joint commission. The commission's job was to recommend how a free election could be organized to establish a democratic government for all Korea. But negotiations between the United States and the Soviet Union did not bring about a compromise. The Soviet Union refused to permit Koreans in their occupied territory north of the 38th parallel to vote in the election held on May 10, 1948. Korea was now divided.

The newly elected Korean National Assembly wrote the nation's first constitution in its four-thousand-year history and elected Syngman Rhee as its president.

South Korean peasants rest beside a road in 1950. Until the Korean War, the country was basically an agricultural society.

The 50,000 American occupation forces gradually began to leave South Korea. Only a 500-man military advisory group was left to help train the Republic of Korea's small army.

In the north, the Soviet Union established a puppet Communist government—the People's Democratic Republic of Korea. However, it was South Korea—the Republic of Korea—which was recognized by the United Nations General Assembly as the only valid government in Korea. Korea had now been divided into two separate countries. There were 9 million Koreans in the more industrialized north and 21 million in the more agricultural south.

After World War II, Americans were eager to come home, take off their uniforms, and pursue a peaceful life. Unfortunately for the democratic countries, Communists—in the Soviet Union and in Asia—saw rich opportunities to gain advantage from the ashes of war. In Europe, the Soviet Union established Communist governments in Poland, Hungary, Bulgaria, Czechoslovakia, Romania, and the eastern part of Germany. What Britain's former prime minister Winston Churchill called "an iron curtain" now divided a democratic Western Europe from Communist Eastern Europe.

While Europe divided itself between East and West, Asia faced a similar situation. In 1949, Communist Chinese forces led by Mao Zedong (Mao Tse-tung) defeated the armies of Chiang Kai-shek, who had been supported by the United States. In October 1949, Mao

U.S. Army occupation troops thumb a ride from a passing jeep as Korean children look on.

proclaimed the People's Republic of China and asked Moscow for Russian support. Chiang and his Nationalist Army retreated to the island of Taiwan, off the Chinese mainland.

In the United States, many people in Congress and the press were critical of the State Department's and President Truman's policies. They felt China had been "lost." Some in Congress advocated sending large shipments of arms or even significant U.S. forces to Korea to bolster the Rhee government. Others argued that with a greatly reduced army and navy, the United States could not police the whole world.

Ominously, in Korea, in the spring of 1950, the "People's Army" of North Korea was making more and more armed raids across the 38th parallel.

2

INVASION

At 9:20 P.M. (Eastern Standard Time) on June 24, 1950, the State Department in Washington received a cablegram from John J. Muccio, the U.S. ambassador in Seoul, Korea: "North Korean forces, consisting of seven divisions and five brigades, with an air force of 100–150 Soviet-made planes crossed the 38th parallel. . . . The ROK forces available for defense number only five divisions, with no air force or armor [tanks]."

Secretary of State Dean Acheson advised President Harry Truman of the invasion. Then he arranged an emergency meeting of the United Nations Security Council through Secretary General Trygve Lie. At the next day's meeting, the Council voted 9 to 0 to condemn the North Korean invasion as a "breach [violation] of the peace." A second resolution, on June 27, made the defense

Two infantrymen of the U.S. Twenty-fourth Division man a machine gun in a defensive position in the first days of the war.

of the Republic of Korea a United Nations war. It called for all members to provide assistance. Eventually, fifteen UN member nations sent combat troops to Korea. Five others sent medical units and other nonmilitary help.

The Korean War would be the only true "UN war" in the organization's history. This was because the Soviet Union, which was a permanent member of the Security Council and could therefore veto any of its actions, boycotted the council's meetings. The Soviets were absent from the council because the UN had recognized the Republic of China (Chiang's Nationalist-controlled government on Taiwan) as a member rather than Communist China on the mainland. The Soviets had created the North Korean regime. If they had been present, they surely would have vetoed the two historic resolutions.

President Truman hastily called together his chief advisers to decide what steps the United States should take. The

On June 17, 1950, the UN Security Council voted to condemn the North Korean invasion of South Korea.

Soviet Union was just across the northern border of the Korean peninsula, and China, with a population of 650 million, was to the peninsula's north and west. Some Americans feared that a conflict in Korea would draw the United States into World War III with either one or both of Korea's powerful neighbors. In March 1949, General Douglas MacArthur had told a reporter that the United States' line of defense in the Pacific "runs through the chain of islands fringing the coast of Asia, from the Philippines through Okinawa . . . [to] Japan and the Aleutian chain to Alaska." He made no mention of the Korean peninsula. Historians have suggested that this had made the Communist nations think the United States would not defend South Korea.

In April 1950, however, worried by increasing criticism for the "loss" of China, President Truman had approved a secret commitment. The commitment

stated that up to 20 percent of the United States' Gross National Product (the total dollar value of all the nation's goods and services) "would be devoted to the military establishment." It also said that "the United States would resist any red [Communist] threat to non-red nations anywhere." These decisions were an expansion of the Truman Doctrine, which the president had first expressed in 1947. This doctrine pledged American support to nations threatened by Communist expansion. If the commitment had been made public, it might have stopped North Korea from invading South Korea.

Now, only two months later, a hard choice had to be made. The president acted decisively. He instructed General MacArthur, his top commander in the Pacific, to make three moves at once.

First, MacArthur was to evacuate all U.S. civilians in South Korea. Second, he was to send all the available arms,

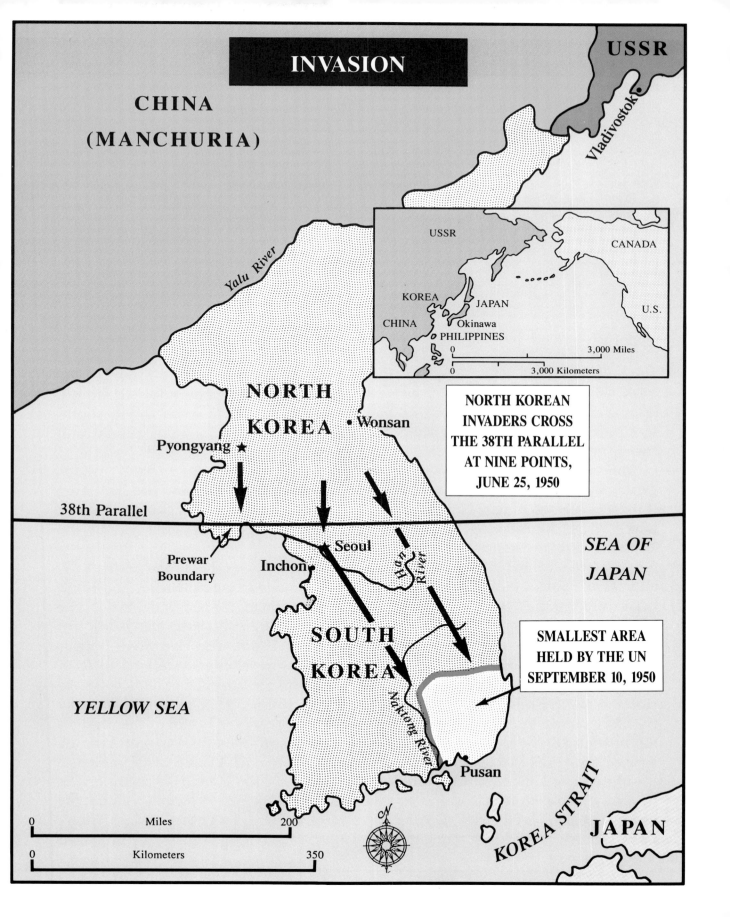

INVASION

CHINA
(MANCHURIA)

USSR

Vladivostok

Yalu River

USSR

KOREA
CHINA

JAPAN

Okinawa
PHILIPPINES

CANADA

U.S.

0   3,000 Miles

0   3,000 Kilometers

NORTH
KOREA

Wonsan

Pyongyang

NORTH KOREAN
INVADERS CROSS
THE 38TH PARALLEL
AT NINE POINTS,
JUNE 25, 1950

38th Parallel

Prewar
Boundary

Inchon

Seoul

Han River

SEA OF
JAPAN

SMALLEST AREA
HELD BY THE UN
SEPTEMBER 10, 1950

SOUTH
KOREA

YELLOW SEA

Naktong River

Pusan

0   Miles   200

0   Kilometers   350

N

KOREA STRAIT

JAPAN

The first U.S. ground troops arrive at the port of Pusan, South Korea.

ammunition, and equipment to the ROK Army. Third, MacArthur's authority was extended to include the U.S. Navy's Seventh Fleet, then patrolling between Taiwan and mainland China.

The situation in Korea was very grave. By 4 A.M. on Sunday morning (June 25, Korean time), North Korean tanks were thundering southward. They met little resistance from the ROK forces between the 38th parallel border and Seoul. Soviet-built Yak warplanes began strafing the South Korean capital on the first day of the invasion. It was a deadly surprise.

The ROK Army ordered a counterattack, sending two divisions to try to stop the North Korean tanks and infantry. They did not succeed. On the morning of June 27, the third day of the invasion, the people of Seoul could hear the thunder of enemy artillery rolling toward them. North Korean planes dropped leaflets on the city, demanding its surrender. The South Korean gov-

ernment had fled from Seoul to the town of Taegu. Thousands of South Koreans clogged the roads going south. The monsoon rains were falling, and the unpaved, muddy roads became so full of refugees that ROK troops couldn't use them. Many people fleeing the invasion couldn't get away from it, and the military couldn't get to the fighting.

Late on the night of June 27, the ROK Army made a tragic mistake. The South Korean forces formed a defensive line on the south bank of the Han River, just south of Seoul. The Han River bridges were to be blown up after the ROK forces on the north bank had crossed to safety. Unfortunately, some ROK Army officers panicked. When the bridges were destroyed at 2:15 A.M. on June 28, they were still loaded with refugees. Some 500 people were blown up on the main bridge or drowned. Hundreds more fell from two other bridges. Moreover, much of the ROK Army remained trapped on the wrong side of the Han River with the enemy fast closing in. They were forced to cross the river in small boats and rafts, losing much of their equipment in the process. The ROK Army lost nearly 44,000 of its 98,000 men, and much of its arms and ammunition, in the crossing.

The North Koreans' swift capture of Seoul was the result of superior forces and the careful planning of the Communist High Command. When the Soviets had occupied North Korea in 1945, Kim Il Sung had been installed as chief of the puppet regime. Kim, a young man who had fought against the Japanese, was trained in Moscow. Many of his generals were also Soviet-trained. Kim's North Korean Army now paused in its advance. The North Koreans needed time to regroup their forces and wait for supplies. They did not make any major attacks until July 5.

Meanwhile, General MacArthur decided to fly from Japan to Korea to see the situation for himself. He landed in Korea on the fourth day of the war. On the ground, one war correspondent with him wrote that they "drove through the swirling, defeated South Korean army and masses of bewildered, pathetic civilian refugees for a firsthand look at the battlefield." What he saw was a nation in collapse.

MacArthur cabled Washington: "The only assurance for holding the present line and the ability to regain lost ground is through the introduction of U.S. combat forces into the Korean battle area." The president authorized MacArthur to

A South Korean civilian took this snapshot of Soviet-made T-34 tanks and North Korean soldiers entering Seoul on June 28, 1950.

Korean civilians clog the roads as the North Korean invaders drive ROK forces south.

23

Two fighter bombers from U.S. Navy Task Force 77 attack the North Korean port of Mokpo early in the war.

do so, and less than twenty hours later the first U.S. infantry units were being flown from Japan to Korea. Truman sent in the troops by executive order, rather than by asking Congress for a declaration of war against North Korea. This is why the Korean War is often called a "police action."

MacArthur had four divisions in Japan, but none of them was at full fighting strength. Few of the troops had combat experience. Most were hardly in fighting trim: the weary veterans of World War II had gone home, leaving mostly raw recruits behind. In one soldier's words, peacetime service in Japan had "consisted mostly of athletics, nightly dances, theater, and Japanese girls. . . . Occupation duty was heaven."

On July 1, the first unit of U.S. troops from the Twenty-fourth Infantry Divi-sion flew into what proved to be "hell." The unit was called Task Force Smith, after its commanding officer, Colonel Charles Smith. The commander of the Twenty-fourth Division, Major General William Dean, ordered Smith: "When you get to Pusan [at the southern end of the Korean peninsula] head for Taejon. We want to stop the North Koreans as far from Pusan as we can. . . . That's all I've got. Good luck to you, and God bless you and your men."

The Americans were met by cheers as they passed through Korean villages on their way to the front. Brigadier General John Church, the senior U.S. adviser to the ROK Army, pointed to a map and told Colonel Smith, "All we need is some men up there who won't run when they see tanks. We're going to move up to support the ROK, and give them moral support."

A carrier-base U.S. Navy F4U Corsair launches its rockets against North Korean troops as UN forces retreat toward Pusan.

On July 5, the Americans took up positions on the Seoul-Pusan highway near the town of Osan, about 30 miles south of Seoul. At just after 8:00 A.M., 10,000 North Korean soldiers and a tank force rolled into view.

Task Force Smith consisted of 540 American soldiers, five 105-millimeter howitzers, and some light mortars and old anti-tank bazookas. The artillery proved almost useless against the North Koreans' Soviet-made T-34 tanks because only a few armor-piercing shells were available. In addition, the bazookas, left over from World War II, did not stop the tanks. One brave lieutenant fired twenty-two bazooka rockets at one T-34, some from a range of only 15 yards, without effect. Task Force Smith managed to knock out four of the thirty-three attacking tanks and killed many enemy infantry, but the Americans were soon overwhelmed by the North Koreans. Some of Colonel Smith's green, untested troops fought bravely. Others broke and ran, abandoning their weapons. Dead and wounded were left behind in the retreat south. In its first day in the war, the United States lost about 150 men killed, wounded, or captured.

Meanwhile, General MacArthur's air and naval forces were having more success. On July 2, on the east coast of Korea, the U.S. cruiser *Juneau* and two British warships destroyed three North Korean torpedo boats and seven small freighters off the port of Chumunjin. This little UN naval victory was the first and only naval "battle" of the war. The three torpedo boats made up the whole of the North Korean navy. UN naval forces controlled both the Korean coastlines on the Yellow Sea and the Sea of Japan throughout the war.

The U.S. Army units that were rushed to Korea from Japan found themselves in combat almost at once. Here, an infantry outpost awaits the enemy in July 1950.

On July 3, fighter and dive bombers from the U.S. and British aircraft carriers launched the first strikes against targets near the North Korean capital of Pyongyang. The first U.S. Air Force engagement of the war took place on June 27. Japan-based Mustangs (propeller planes) and Shooting Stars (jets) shot down six Soviet-built Yak fighter planes. By mid-July, most of the North Korean Air Force had been destroyed, largely caught on the ground.

The land war was still going very badly, however. There was nothing yet in Korea that seemed able to stop the onslaught of the enemy's T-34 tanks.

The defeat of Task Force Smith on the road at Osan boosted enemy morale and badly hurt the Americans' spirit. One GI said, "Everyone thought they would turn around and go back when

they found out who they were fighting." General Dean told General MacArthur that U.S. estimates of the North Korean soldier's training, equipment, and fighting ability had been "underestimated."

Evidence of this fact continued to come. The pattern all across the width of the peninsula was the same. U.S. and ROK units were trying to buy time as reinforcements came from Japan and the mainland United States. They succeeded, but just barely and with heavy losses—including General Dean, who was captured after the North Koreans took the town of Taejon on July 21.

The Korean War was a conflict of countless small, bloody battles. At this early stage of the struggle, the war was fought mainly along the Seoul-Pusan highway. At point after point, UN forces put up defensive blocking positions. The UN troops fought as long as possible against the North Korean tanks, and retreated when enemy infantry outflanked—got around—their positions.

By the end of July 1950, the UN Eighth Army—now under the direct command of Major General Walton Walker—had retreated into a circular defensive line around the southeastern port of Pusan. This area was about 50 miles wide and 90 miles deep. Crowded into this toehold, which was called the Pusan Perimeter, were some 95,000 U.S. troops and 45,000 ROK soldiers.

General Walker told his embattled men:

Many inexperienced U.S. troops suffered heavy casualties. Here, a wounded GI is comforted by a buddy as a casualty tag is made out.

We are fighting against time. There will be no more retreating. There is no line behind us to which we can retreat. . . . We must fight until the end. Any man who gives ground may be personally responsible for the deaths of thousands of his comrades. I want everybody to understand that we are going to hold this line. We are going to win.

3

INCHON: A CLASSIC COUNTERATTACK

As July 1951 turned to August, the United Nations forces were battered back by the North Korean forces all across the peninsula. The UN commanding officer, General Walton Walker, was handicapped by his soldiers' lack of battle experience. Many of his officers and men had no desire to fight in this "police action." Sometimes whole units of infantry would "bug out"—retreat from their positions.

But by late summer, reinforcements were pouring into the port of Pusan. These new troops included U.S. Marines, among them many veterans of World War II. Soon, UN forces defending the southernmost part of Korea numbered about 114,000 soldiers and marines.

General Walker told Marine Brigadier General Edward Craig that his men

A U.S. Army Pershing medium tank roars north on road above Seoul after the successful UN landing at Inchon.

would be used as "troubleshooters" to stop attacks along the UN defense line. This line, the Pusan Perimeter, ran along the Naktong River in the west, turned east just above the city of Taegu, and stopped on the east coast.

General Craig told his men, "The Pusan Perimeter is like a weakened dike and we will be used to plug holes in it as they open. It will be costly fighting against a numerically superior enemy." Then he reminded them, "The marines have never lost a battle. This brigade will not be the first."

In the first three weeks of August the North Koreans made many unsuccessful attempts to break through the UN line and capture Pusan. Then, in early August, the marines counterattacked and pushed the enemy back 16 miles. Marine Corsair fighter-bombers, which flew in from aircraft carriers, gave close support to the UN ground forces. Armed with a 500-pound bomb or a tank of napalm (jellied gasoline) and

General Douglas MacArthur's amphibious landing at Inchon on September 15, 1950 (shown here), was one of the most effective military operations in history.

machine guns, the Corsairs wrecked North Korean tanks and supply columns and attacked enemy positions. They took a heavy toll.

But the Eighth Army, the major UN force, was still on the defensive. On August 15, the North Koreans managed to cross the Naktong River. The North Koreans captured a platoon of Americans in the battle. The prisoners were herded into a gully and machine-gunned. Twenty-six died, but a few escaped and lived to tell the tale. A furious General MacArthur ordered leaflets dropped by UN planes. They warned the North Koreans that their leaders would be held responsible for such war crimes.

On August 29, the first non-U.S. ground force from a UN member nation arrived—the British 27th Brigade from Hong Kong. They were just in time. The North Koreans launched a final all-out attack on the Pusan Perimeter three days later. The North Koreans had about 100,000 men, but they had only about 100 tanks left, thanks to UN air support.

The enemy attacked all around the Pusan Perimeter. One bloodstained mountain ridge changed hands thirteen times in less than a month as it passed from the UN to the North Korean forces and back. General Walker gave some ground before once again using his marine "troubleshooter" brigade and battle-seasoned Twenty-fourth Division to stop the advance. By September, the Communist offensive was all but over.

Meanwhile, back in General MacArthur's Tokyo headquarters and in Washington, military and naval staffs were working at a frantic pace. They were planning a great offensive that was to reverse the course of the war.

On June 29, when he had flown into

Korea for an inspection, General MacArthur had realized that he needed time to get reinforcements and arms to the peninsula. He decided to trade land for time. The UN forces retreated gradually to the south. Meanwhile, the navy and air force bombed and shelled the North Koreans without letup.

As the enemy moved south—capturing Seoul and Taejon and finally threatening Taegu and Pusan—the North Korean supply lines grew longer and longer. Because there were few good highways and rail lines in Korea, the North Korean supply routes were vulnerable to UN air attack.

The masterstroke in MacArthur's plan was a daring amphibious attack on Inchon, the port city for Seoul, in September. Inchon was about 150 miles behind the front lines around Taegu and Pusan. The general knew that a surprise

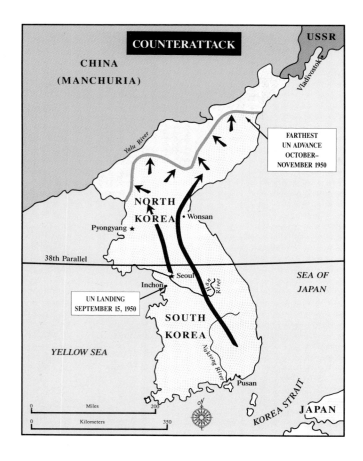

COUNTERATTACK

CHINA (MANCHURIA)

USSR

Vladivostok

Yalu River

FARTHEST
UN ADVANCE
OCTOBER–
NOVEMBER 1950

NORTH
KOREA

• Wonsan

Pyongyang ★

38th Parallel

Seoul

Inchon

Han River

SEA OF
JAPAN

UN LANDING
SEPTEMBER 15, 1950

SOUTH

KOREA

Naktong River

YELLOW SEA

Miles   0   200

Kilometers   0   350

Pusan

KOREA STRAIT   JAPAN

attack would hurt the enemy both psychologically and physically. The North Koreans, a long way from home, would have a natural fear of being cut off from the north and being trapped by the enemy. By landing at Inchon, the UN forces could recapture Seoul. The capital city had the best airfield in the country, and it was the hub of Korea's road and rail system. More important, landing behind the lines would force the North Koreans to fight in two places at once.

In July, MacArthur had announced his plan to his superiors—the Joint Chiefs of Staff of all the services. The top commanders in Washington, General Omar Bradley and General Lawton Collins, turned down the plan at first. The navy, which would be responsible for landing the attacking force, was doubtful about the choice of Inchon. Rear Admiral James Doyle, who would direct the landing, described the many problems.

First, Inchon had no beaches, only piers and seawalls. The surrounding waters could be easily mined. The approaches to the little harbor were difficult for a large fleet to maneuver in. Worst of all was the problem of the tides, which sometimes rose as much as 36 feet at high tide.

One doubtful general gloomily called the Inchon attack "a 5,000-to-1 shot."

LSTs (Landing Ship-Tanks) unload UN equipment at Inchon on September 15, 1950.

But General MacArthur's arguments finally won out, and the attack was scheduled for the first high tide on September 15.

At dawn on that day, a fleet of more than 260 vessels was in position off Inchon. UN planes and naval guns blasted the harbor defenses with rockets, bombs, and shells. At 6:30 A.M., the first landing craft put a battalion of marines ashore on Wolmi Island, just offshore from Inchon. Wolmi had heavy guns that had to be put out of action. This was done in less than two hours, with only seventeen marines wounded. General MacArthur watched the landings from a ship offshore. When he saw the American flag flying over Wolmi, the general wrote a message to the naval commander, "The Navy and Marines have never shone more brightly than this morning."

Later that day, at the evening high tide, other marine units attacked two more points on the coast. Both landing points were seawalls, and the marines had to get ashore by clambering up ladders. The UN forces quickly advanced inland, meeting only minor North Korean resistance. By September 26, Seoul was in UN hands. The landing had been a brilliant stroke that totally surprised the North Koreans.

The famous U.S. Admiral William "Bull" Halsey called Inchon "the most masterly and audacious strategic strike in all history." A great victory had been won. The UN had defeated between 30,000 and 40,000 of the enemy at a cost

U.S. Marines endured intense house-to-house combat in the battle to recapture Seoul in September 1950.

General Douglas MacArthur, UN supreme commander, greets ROK president Syngman Rhee at Seoul's Kimpo airport as the president visits the newly liberated South Korean capital.

of 536 dead, 2,550 wounded, and 65 missing.

There was a disturbing discovery at Kimpo airfield, however. General James Gavin, who was evaluating the enemy's weapons and systems, reported that the North Koreans had made many improvements to the field. According to Gavin, "Sophisticated thinking had gone into the planning . . . in anticipation of using the airfield by a modern air force." He believed that an intervention by the Chinese seemed very likely.

Meanwhile, to the south, the UN forces around Taegu and Pusan launched a major offensive. They broke out of their defensive positions and began pushing the North Koreans back into the UN troops moving south from Inchon. The offensive's goal was to destroy the thirteen enemy divisions caught between the two UN forces.

By late September, the North Korean Army had been almost shattered. Tens of thousands of North Koreans surrendered. Some took refuge in the mountains, where they formed guerrilla bands that would harass the UN for many months to come. But most of the retreating North Koreans struggled to get back north to defend their homeland.

The fighting, both in North and South Korea, had caused great misery for the Korean people. A Canadian officer described conditions in the war-torn peninsula: "Everything had been beaten down to the lowest level. . . . The place was a huge armed camp, strewn with homeless children and dev-

British Commonwealth Brigade troops mounted on U.S. Army tanks drive into North Korea.

astation." Thousands of Korean civilians had been killed and hundreds of thousands more made homeless. The advancing UN troops found grim evidence of what life after Communist "liberation" was like. In the South Korean town of Sachon, the North Koreans had herded 280 South Korean police, government officials, and other civilians into a jail and then burned it to the ground. Between 5,000 and 7,000 civilians were murdered around Taejon, along with at least forty American soldiers.

The Korean police action was now only ninety days old, but MacArthur's brilliant counteroffensive had recovered the Republic of Korea's land south of the 38th parallel. The question now was whether the UN forces should pursue the war farther north of the border between the two Koreas.

ROK President Syngman Rhee said: "Where is the 38th parallel? It is nonexistent. I am going all the way to the Yalu River [the border between North

Korea and Chinese Manchuria], and the United Nations can't stop me." The UN did not try. On October 6, the General Assembly of the United Nations agreed to let UN troops cross into North Korea to carry out the "destruction of the North Korean Armed Forces."

By mid-October, UN forces had advanced 20 miles into North Korean territory. Communist Premier Kim Il Sung ordered his weary troops to defend Pyongyang, the North Korean capital, to the last man. But on October 19, the U.S. First Cavalry Division and the ROK First Division captured Pyongyang.

MacArthur then ordered an airborne landing of the 187th Airborne Regiment, complete with vehicles and artillery, about 30 miles beyond the Communist capital. Marine and army units made amphibious landings on the North Korean coast, trapping the retreating North Korean forces. The UN took about 135,000 North Korean prisoners. As October came to an end, a ROK unit reached the Yalu River.

But President Truman, and many people in the UN, had become concerned by the possibility of a Chinese entry to "save" their North Korean allies. China's Foreign Minister, Zhou Enlai (Chou En-lai), had warned: "The Chinese people absolutely will not tolerate foreign aggression, nor will they tolerate seeing their neighbors savagely invaded by the imperialists."

On October 15, President Truman flew to Wake Island in the Pacific to meet with General MacArthur. He

A crying child, separated from her parents in war-ravaged Seoul, presents a classic condemnation of the horrors of war.

awarded MacArthur his fifth Distinguished Service Medal and asked what the general believed the Chinese would do.

MacArthur reported, "I believe that formal resistance will end throughout North Korea by Thanksgiving. It is my hope to be able to withdraw the [UN] army to Japan by Christmas." The Chinese, he said, had "probably no more than 100–125,000 men distributed along the Yalu River. They have no Air Force. Now that we have bases for our Air Force in Korea, if the Chinese tried to get down to Pyongyang, there would be the greatest slaughter."

There was indeed to be great slaughter, for both the UN and the Communists, in the barren mountains of Korea. As MacArthur was reporting to Truman on Wake Island, more than 180,000 Chinese troops began crossing the Yalu River into North Korea.

THE MOVIE WAR

The Korean War is often called the "forgotten war." To many Americans, it was a remote conflict. The public had largely lost interest in the conflict after the winter of 1950. Korea seemed to be an endless story of battles and peace talks that accomplished little. Television journalism was in its infancy in the early 1950s. The war was not in America's living room night after night, as was the Vietnam War more than a decade later.

The war that was fought on that far-off peninsula would be even less a part of America's memory if it were not the setting for four excellent movies.

Much of what we know of military history has come down to us through "stories." Storytellers—from the playwrights of ancient Greece to modern writers and filmmakers—can get underneath the facts and give us a sense of human emotions in wartime.

The cast of the M.A.S.H. *television series in a "family portrait."*

Gregory Peck, right, played the courageous infantry company commander in the 1959 film Pork Chop Hill.

MOVIE STAR NEWS

M.A.S.H. stands for Mobile Army Surgical Hospital. It was the title of a popular 1970 movie and an even more popular television series that ran for eleven years. The comedy chronicled the often funny, sometimes grim life of the doctors, nurses, and troops who pass through a front line hospital. In their spare time, the surgeons and nurses rebel against the army's strict rules. Critic Judith Crist wrote of the *M.A.S.H.* TV series: "The humor is blood-soaked and cloaks a bitter and horrible truth." Alan Alda, the show's star, insisted that no episode of *M.A.S.H.* could be filmed without a hospital scene to remind viewers of the horrors of war.

Pork Chop Hill is a realistic 1959 film. It tells the story of an infantry company that is given the task of taking an important hill in the "Iron Triangle" north of Seoul. The men, many of whom are almost eligible to go home, are bitter about risking their lives day after day while the truce talks drone on.

The Bridges at Toko-Ri, a 1954 film adapted from a novel by James Michener, is about the air war fought from navy carriers off North Korea. The movie portrays comradeship among navy pilots, many of them veterans of World War II who have been called back to service to fight, and sometimes die, in Korea.

The Manchurian Candidate is a spy thriller. An American war hero returns home "brainwashed" by his Communist captors to kill a leading politician. Critics have described the movie as "insanely plotted but brilliantly handled" and "intelligent, funny, and superbly written and beautifully played."

In a scene from The Bridges at Toko-Ri, *William Holden, a carrier-based pilot, and his task-force admiral, Frederick March, try to comfort a flyer's distraught wife, played by Grace Kelly.*

Communist soldiers carry wounded U.S. soldiers into captivity in The Manchurian Candidate, *a thriller about a "brainwashed" American veteran programmed for assassination.*

TO THE YALU
AND BACK TO THE HAN

The first contact with the Chinese came on October 25, 1950, at two points along the northern edge of the eastern front. A South Korean battalion that had advanced to the Yalu River was virtually wiped out at a Chinese roadblock. Next, the Chinese hit other ROK units. One regiment of 3,552 soldiers was trapped, and only 875 soldiers escaped. A British unit also had a firefight with a force they identified as Chinese. By October 31, the UN had taken 25 Chinese prisoners. Then, on November 1, the U.S. First Cavalry Division—which had long since phased out its own horse units—was attacked by Chinese cavalry on Mongolian ponies.

On that same day, the first Communist jets—Russian-built MIG-15s—appeared over the battlefront. At first, the UN pilots were startled because their F-

In the mountainous battlefields of Korea, wounded were brought down for evacuation to hospitals by the Korean Service Corps (South Koreans assigned to U.S. combat units).

80 Shooting Stars were outclassed by the MIGs. In December, however, the first unit of new F-86 Sabre jets arrived. The UN was able to keep control of the air.

There was now no doubt that China had entered the war. On November 5, General MacArthur reported the Chinese intervention to the United Nations. He described the MIGs and the identification of prisoners from the "Chinese People's Volunteers." MacArthur warned of the "alien Communist forces" massing across the Yalu. The general called China's action a "possible trap . . . a new and fresh army facing us."

Both North Korea and China responded to MacArthur's message. North Korean Premier Kim Il Sung's government admitted "participation" by Chinese "volunteers." Beijing (Peking) said that if it is the "Chinese people's will to assist Korea and resist American aggression . . . the People's

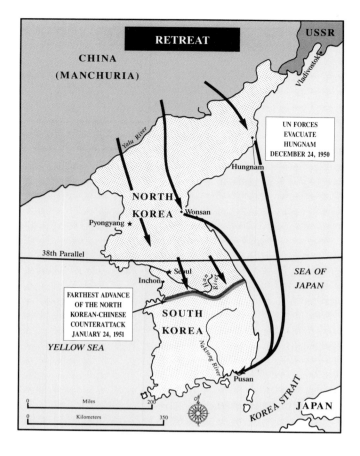

RETREAT

CHINA
(MANCHURIA)

USSR

Vladivostok

Yalu River

UN FORCES
EVACUATE
HUNGNAM
DECEMBER 24, 1950

Hungnam

NORTH
KOREA

Wonsan

Pyongyang ★

38th Parallel

Seoul

Inchon

Han River

SEA OF
JAPAN

FARTHEST ADVANCE
OF THE NORTH
KOREAN-CHINESE
COUNTERATTACK
JANUARY 24, 1951

SOUTH
KOREA

YELLOW SEA

Naktong River

Pusan

KOREA STRAIT

JAPAN

Miles 200

Kilometers 350

Government of China sees no reason to prevent their departure for Korea."

Then, for over two weeks, there was an eerie lull in the fighting. UN troops were not under attack. Patrols reported that the enemy seemed to have withdrawn as heavy snows covered North Korea.

At this point General MacArthur made a fateful decision. He decided not to pull his troops back from the Yalu. On November 9, he wrote his superiors: "I believe that with my air power . . . I can deny reinforcements coming across the Yalu." MacArthur also said that he could destroy the enemy forces already in North Korea.

The biggest problem was that Mac-Arthur believed his staff's estimate that the UN forces faced about 100,000 Communists—30,000–40,000 North Koreans and 60,000–70,000 Chinese. In fact, there were about 300,000 Chinese facing the UN forces. These soldiers were not untrained volunteers but well-trained troops from the Third and Fourth Chinese Field Armies.

At the end of November, UN land forces in Korea numbered about 205,000 men. Fresh units arrived from several UN member nations: the U.S. Third Infantry Division, another British brigade, a Turkish brigade, and battalions from Canada, Thailand, the Philippines, and the Netherlands. MacArthur's naval and air forces numbered about 85,000

General MacArthur's forces resumed their offensive, which he believed would quickly end the war. His plan was to attack northward on both sides of the high mountain range that runs north-south, dividing the Korean peninsula. Lieutenant General Walton Walker was in command of the UN's Eighth Army on the west and central fronts. Major General Edward M. Almond commanded the X Corps in the east. A gap of more than 50 miles separated the two commands at some points. This was a major problem in the fighting that followed.

At first, on November 24 and 25, the Eighth Army was able to advance. But suddenly, on the night of the 25th, hordes of Chinese troops battered the ROK II Corps, one of the weakest points on the Eighth Army front. The ROK

An aerial view of the rugged terrain around the Chosin Reservoir.

forces gave ground, and soon the U.S. Second Division retreated as well. To the east, the X Corps wasn't scheduled to launch the big UN offensive until November 27. The U.S. First Marine Division was positioned on the southern and western sides of the Chosin Reservoir, and the U.S. Seventh Infantry Division was on its eastern side.

As the Eighth Army units began to fall back, the X Corps was left vulnerable to attack. It was known that many Chinese were in the frozen mountains. Soon the Chinese began moving in behind the X Corps. By now there were hundreds of thousands of Chinese troops in Korea. They had moved in at night, unseen by the UN aircraft reconnaissance (spotter) planes watching for enemy movements. The Chinese troops were tough and well disciplined. One unit marched, on foot, at night, 286 miles from Manchuria down into Korea in sixteen days—averaging 16 miles a day over very difficult ground. The human waves of Chinese swarmed over ROK and U.S. defenses alike.

General Walker tried to strengthen his lines by adding reserve units. However, the masses of Chinese couldn't be stopped. The Eighth Army began a general retreat. The roads to the south became clogged by thousands of civilian refugees, soldiers, and vehicles.

The Chinese developed a standard attack plan that worked all too well. They made direct attacks on the UN line and slipped infantry through or around UN weak points at the same time. Then they set up roadblocks behind the UN lines. The Chinese also dug in along the roadside to harass the retreating forces with rifles, machine guns, and mortars. The plan was carried out with deadly accuracy.

U.S. infantrymen man a forward position in the bitter cold of December 1950.

U.S. troops advancing toward the Yalu River behind U.S. air attacks.

The U.S. Second Infantry Division was ordered to fight a rear-guard action. Their mission was to buy time for the rest of the Eighth Army to fall back to the Chongchon River. On December 1, about 7,000 Second Division troops, in a truck convoy, headed south toward Sunchon. They drove into an ambush that survivors called a "living hell." The Chinese were in position on either side of a five-mile stretch of road called the "gauntlet." Some enemy guns were as close as 100 yards from the convoy.

One soldier, Private Kenneth Poss, recalled: "The Chinese hit us from both sides. The road was clogged with every imaginable type of vehicle—jeeps, trucks of all sizes, tanks, and artillery. . . . They would let the tanks go by, then close in behind them. They'd knock out the lead vehicle, then beat hell out of us as we tried to push it off the road." Private Poss was among the lucky soldiers who walked out of the

trap; of the 7,000 troops in the convoy, roughly 3,000 were killed or wounded. Newspaper columnist Walter Winchell wrote at the time: "If you have a son overseas, write to him. If you have a son in the 2nd Division, pray for him."

Things were no better on the eastern front, over the mountains dividing the peninsula. Major General Oliver Smith, commander of the marines, complained about his "wide open left flank." The marines were strung out "along a single mountain road for 120 air miles from Hamhung to the border."

Six Chinese divisions attacked the UN forces; at first the American forces did not retreat. On December 1, the UN commanders ordered the X Corps to make a fighting retreat to the east coast. The navy would evacuate the troops from the port of Hungnam.

None of the troops in the field was sorry to go. The temperature in the mountains got down to as low as 35 degrees below zero at night. Food, weapons, and human flesh often froze. Frozen rations had to be chipped out of cans with bayonet tips. Many troops suffered frostbite. Between December 1 and 4, two marine regiments, supported by heavy air attacks, fought their way out. They suffered 1,500 casualties but escaped being trapped. But the Chinese were still there.

It was at this grim time that the First Marine Division commander told some war correspondents, "Gentlemen, we are not retreating. We are merely advancing in another direction."

In fact, General Smith could have chosen to evacuate his 14,000 remaining troops by air. But rather than leaving behind the division's heavy equipment, he chose to fight his way through the remaining bloody miles to the coast.

It was a tough fight. Korea's mountainous geography favored the attacking Chinese. The marines had to keep to the narrow mountain roads, giving the enemy the opportunity to fire on their flanks. Rockslides and roadblocks sometimes held the marine columns up until engineers could blast a path through them. The bitter cold was as fierce an enemy as the Chinese. Vehicles took hours to start, and oil sometimes turned to mush in their engines. Howling winds and snowstorms added to the marines' misery.

Fighting from one jagged ridge to the next, the marines managed to push the Chinese out of their path. The Chinese soldiers earned the marines' respect. They sometimes found the Chinese fro-

A woodcut by Chinese artist Li Hua is captioned "Chinese People's Volunteers in Korea capture U.S. tanks."

zen to death in their defensive positions. Those still alive fought fiercely.

But somehow, thirteen days after being cut off, the marines began to march into the port of Hungnam on December 10. The 193 ships of the UN fleet awaited them. By December 24, unit by unit, some 100,000 UN soldiers and marines and 98,000 Korean civilians had boarded the ships and sailed south down the Korean peninsula to Pusan.

The marines' fighting retreat from the Chosin Reservoir had been heroic. They had brought out their wounded, most of their dead, and their equipment. But as engineers blew up Hungnam, those on the departing ships realized that the Chinese had driven the X Corps out of North Korea.

MacArthur's plan for the Eighth Army was to establish a defensive front along a road crossing the peninsula from Pyongyang to the Sea of Japan port

Off the Korean coast, the battleship Missouri *fires its guns in support of the embattled troops inland.*

of Wonson. But Pyongyang, the North Korean capital, was abandoned on December 5. By mid-December this line had been pierced at other points by the Chinese and North Korean forces. The next defense line for the Eighth Army was now north and east of Seoul.

On December 23, General Walton Walker, the Eighth Army commander, died in a jeep accident. He was replaced by Lieutenant General Matthew Ridgway.

The Communists didn't give the new commander a chance to settle in. On New Year's Eve, they launched an assault on two ROK divisions north of Seoul. Ridgway's reserves stopped the Communists but lost ground. The general pulled his troops back to the south side of the Han River, again leaving Seoul to the enemy, who captured it on January 4, 1951.

The UN's new defensive line across the peninsula was called the D Line. It was as far south as the UN troops would be pushed in the war. While it seemed that the Communists' early 1951 offensive had gained them much ground, it had also dangerously extended their supply lines. Once again, whenever the winter skies were clear, the UN air force—the U.S. Fifth Air Force and navy planes—blasted the Communists. In the first half of January, the Communists suffered an estimated 38,000 casualties. More than half of these were caused by the bombing and strafing by the air force. The UN lost about 13,000 men killed, wounded, and missing in this period.

Navy carriers heel over into the wind as they turn to receive planes returning from a mission supporting UN ground forces.

By January 15, General Ridgway was able to begin offensive operations again, pushing north as far as Suwon. The Communists had been weakened by the pounding from the air and UN firepower on the ground. On January 25, Ridgway's Eighth Army began Operation Thunderbolt, an offensive that pushed the Communists back to the Han River.

In February, the port of Inchon, and Kimpo, Seoul's airfield, were both back in UN hands. But Seoul did not fall to the UN until March 14, after the bitter battles of Operation Ripper. This offensive pushed north on all fronts and included an airborne attack by the 187th Airborne Regiment. The paratroopers dropped at Munsan, in an attempt to trap a North Korean force between Seoul and Kaesong. The enemy escaped this trap. By the beginning of April, however, UN forces had advanced a few miles beyond the 38th parallel. The Korean War—or police action—was roughly back where it had started.

A wounded U.S. Second Division infantryman (left), captured and released by the advancing Chinese, is helped back to UN lines by an Australian marine.

5

STALEMATE, TALKS,
AND TRUCE

All wars are fought both on the battle-field and in the legislatures of the governments involved. The Korean War was no exception. Almost from the war's start, President Harry Truman and his Joint Chiefs of Staff, headed by General Omar Bradley, had disagreements with UN commander General Douglas MacArthur. These disagreements had their roots in American foreign policy in the years following World War II.

When the cold war (the post–World War II conflict between Communist and non-Communist nations) began, President Truman had firmly stated that Communist expansion should be resisted throughout the world. But by 1950, the Soviet Union had installed Communist governments in much of Eastern Europe. In Asia, China, with one-fourth of the world's population,

had fallen to Mao Zedong's Communist forces in 1949.

Some Republicans in Congress pointed to these Communist successes and accused the Democratic Truman administration of being "soft on communism." (Actually, the administration had successfully supported anti-Communist forces in Greece and Turkey.) But in 1950, being "hard on communism" was difficult. The American armed forces had been much reduced after World War II. They were not strong enough to fight even "limited" wars in two places at once. Also, U.S. policy was aimed at containing Communist expansion in Europe, rather than in Asia. Finally, in a world where atomic bombs were in both American and Soviet hands, a third world war was a horrifying possibility. Any military action had to be undertaken cautiously.

MacArthur felt Washington wasn't allowing him to conduct the war in Korea as aggressively as he needed to in order to win. MacArthur wanted to

The MLR (main line of resistance) during the battle of the hills in October 1952.

THE HARRY S. TRUMAN LIBRARY

General Douglas MacArthur greets President Harry S. Truman at their meeting on Wake Island.

bomb Chinese supply lines in Manchuria and impose a naval blockade of China's coast. He also wanted to "release" Nationalist Chinese forces on Taiwan to attack the mainland and, perhaps, to fight in Korea.

The general's superiors in Washington felt any of these moves could broaden the war. They feared such actions might lead the Soviet Union to enter the war on the side of its Communist allies. The administration felt it was better to seek a negotiated peace than to continue the loss of troops and military hardware in Korea. MacArthur, of course, disagreed.

On January 13, 1951, the United Nations General Assembly voted for an immediate cease-fire in Korea. The UN proposed a withdrawal of all "non-Korean" troops. The withdrawal would be supervised by a UN-approved administration. But the Chinese rejected the UN proposal, and the fighting continued.

The disagreement between Truman and MacArthur also continued. It came to the boiling point when the general wrote to a Republican congressman who had criticized Truman's war policy. MacArthur wrote that Europe should not be given priority over Asia. "There is no substitute for victory," he said. The general was openly defying his commander in chief, the U.S. president.

That did it. With the policy of the president questioned in this way, President Truman felt he had no choice. On April 11, 1951, he relieved MacArthur of his command, replacing him with General Matthew Ridgway.

General MacArthur was one of the great figures of U.S. military history. His dismissal caused a storm of protest, from both Truman's critics in Congress and the American public. Angry telegrams and letters poured into the White House. One senator demanded the removal of Secretary of State Dean Acheson and the impeachment of President Truman.

General MacArthur returned home to a hero's tickertape parade in New York. On April 19, 1951, he addressed a joint session of Congress. He again called for an economic and naval blockade of China, air operations north of the Yalu River, and the use of Nationalist Chinese forces. In an emotional close to his speech, MacArthur looked back on his fifty-two years of military service. He recalled an old army ballad that proclaimed, "Old soldiers never die, they

U.S. troops advance cautiously after an airstrike on an enemy position.

just fade away." "I now close my military career," said MacArthur, "and just fade away, an old soldier who tried to do his duty as God gave him the light to see that duty. Goodbye."

Some military leaders supported the general's position on Korea, but others did not. All the Joint Chiefs of Staff voted for MacArthur's dismissal. General Omar Bradley reminded Americans, "In the opinion of the Joint Chiefs of Staff, [MacArthur's] strategy would involve us in the wrong war, at the wrong place, at the wrong time, and with the wrong enemy."

These were sobering words. Public opinion began to swing toward the Truman administration's policy of "containing," or holding in check, the enemy. That way both sides could work toward a negotiated peace that would preserve South Korea's freedom.

President-elect Dwight D. Eisenhower, right, with UN commander General James van Fleet, center, and the British Commonwealth Division commander.

49

In the meantime, on April 14, Lieutenant General James Van Fleet took command of the UN Eighth Army while Ridgway moved up to overall UN command. Van Fleet was given a memorandum titled "Prevention of War with the Soviet Union." It instructed him to "repel aggression against so much of the territory (and the people therein) of the Republic of Korea as you now occupy." The UN goal was no longer to "liberate" or "unify" the two Koreas, but only to stop the enemy from advancing.

The Communists launched a major offensive on April 22, once again beginning with an attack on a South Korean division. The South Koreans retreated. Van Fleet pulled his forces back to strongly fortified positions north of Seoul called the No-Name Line. In May, new Communist attacks pushed the Eighth Army's eastern front south of the

38th parallel for the third time. Van Fleet's forces rallied, however, and began an advance that at some points pushed as much as 20 miles into North Korean territory.

Air support by air force, navy, and marine aircraft continued to hurt the Communist forces and their supply lines. During the last weeks of May, the enemy suffered very heavy casualties. General Van Fleet reported his forces had taken more than 10,000 prisoners in a single week. As the first year of the war ended, the UN estimated that the North Koreans had suffered 600,000 casualties and the Chinese had lost close to half a million men.

On June 23, 1951, the Soviet delegate to the United Nations proposed beginning discussions aimed at achieving a cease-fire agreement and an armistice (a truce, or agreement to stop fighting

Soldiers of the U.S. Twenty-fifth Division struggle for cover during an enemy bombardment in April 1951.

temporarily). General Ridgway broadcast an invitation to the Communists to meet. They accepted, and on July 10 truce talks began at the village of Kaesong near the 38th parallel. The talks later moved to another village, Panmunjom.

The Communists' chief negotiator was North Korean General Nam Il. American Vice Admiral Turner Joy led the UN group. At first, the Communists used the talks as an opportunity to launch propaganda attacks on South Korea and the United States. They made wild statements about "the murderer Rhee" and "capitalist U.S. thugs" and accused the Americans of conducting "germ warfare."

The talks broke off several times. But in November 1951, Washington ordered General Van Fleet not to begin any major operations. The UN then made a proposal to the Communist negotiators. If they agreed to an armistice within thirty days, the existing front would be made the final line between the two sides. During this lull in the fighting, the Communists resupplied their forces and strengthened their defenses across the peninsula.

As 1951 passed and 1952 began, the American public became increasingly discouraged by the continuing casualties in this "limited" but bloody war. Korea was a major issue in the 1952 presidential election. General Dwight D. Eisenhower, the Republican candidate, announced, "I shall go to Korea." American voters took this to mean that if "Ike" was elected he would end the

Medical corpsmen unload a wounded man at a field (MASH) hospital.

war in Korea one way or another. President Truman did not run for reelection. The Democrats chose Adlai Stevenson as their candidate.

After his victory over Stevenson in November, President-elect Eisenhower did travel to the war zone. There, he met with UN commanders and ROK President Syngman Rhee and reviewed the situation.

One of the stickiest issues that prevented agreement in the truce talks was the problem of prisoners of war. The UN forces held 132,000 North Korean and Chinese prisoners, while about 100,000 UN troops were in Communist hands. Over 11,000 American troops were missing and believed to be captured. However, the Communists claimed they held only about 3,200 Americans and 7,000 South Koreans.

This lack of agreement in numbers created a major problem. There was another problem. Many of the North Korean and Chinese troops held prisoner by the UN forces didn't want to be returned to their Communist homelands.

A survey of prisoners held by the UN revealed that over 40 percent of the Communist troops did not want to go home. This was a humiliating "loss of face" for North Korea and China. A war-within-a-war broke out in UN POW camps as strict Communists rioted and killed fellow soldiers who wished to stay in South Korea. The worst incident took place in the big POW camp on the island of Koje. One American guard and 75 prisoners were killed before UN forces restored order.

President Truman had pledged, "We will not buy an armistice by turning over human beings for slaughter and slavery." President Eisenhower also agreed not to force unwilling prisoners to return to Communist rule. The talks were broken off once again. But the Eisenhower administration had also begun to send stern warnings to the Communists. After the war, Secretary of Defense John Foster Dulles revealed that the United States had asked the government of India to pass a message on to the Soviet Union. The message asked the Soviets to advise North Korea and China that the United States would, if necessary, use atomic weapons to end the war.

In September and October 1952, the Communists launched heavy attacks on UN positions north of Seoul. But the UN forces held on.

In early 1953, the peace talks started again. On April 20, there was an exchange of sick prisoners of war. Over 6,000 ailing Communist troops were exchanged for 684 UN soldiers. The war's end seemed in sight. Then ROK President Syngman Rhee stated that he would continue fighting without UN support if a single Chinese Communist remained in North Korea. Despite this last-minute threat, the United Nations and the Communists signed a cease-fire agreement on July 27, 1953. The big guns were finally silent after three years, one month, and two days of war. But, sadly, the Land of the Morning Calm was to remain a troubled—and sometimes bloody—land for decades to come.

Many have noted that the Korean War was the first important military conflict that the United States undertook that it didn't clearly win. American General Mark Clark, UN commander at the war's end, remarked, "I cannot find it in me to exult in this hour," as he signed the cease-fire agreement. Critics of the war's conduct, who echoed MacArthur's belief that "there is no substitute for victory," asked, "What did we achieve, and at what cost?"

The costs were indeed high. The Korean people—in both North and South Korea—suffered an estimated *two million* civilian casualties, a number equal to the population of West Virginia. The ROK Army had casualties of about 844,000, and the North Korean military forces had casualties estimated at 624,000. The value of property destroyed in South Korea alone was more

Three North Korean delegates examine maps at the Panmunjom truce talks.

But this "limited" war did achieve several important things. The Korean War was a turning point in both American and world history. The conflict marked the first time that a world organization had acted with unity and courage to resist one nation's aggression against another. The United Nations, and the United States, had shown restraint in a dangerous world. But they had saved Syngman Rhee's young nation from being taken over by Communist North Korea. Today, more than 45 million citizens of an independent and prosperous South Korea see that as no "limited" victory.

than a billion dollars. The United States spent almost $7 billion on the three-year war effort.

As for the non-Korean forces, Chinese casualties are believed to have numbered about 960,000. Casualties among the 15 UN member nations other than the United States were 17,260 killed and wounded. The United States had 33,629 men killed (enough to fill a football stadium) and 103,284 wounded. Even those who survived the fighting paid a price. While most people in the United States supported the war, they had quickly tired of hearing about it. When U.S. servicemen and women returned home, there were few parades for them. Also, veterans of the fighting in Korea received fewer government benefits than veterans of World War II. It was not until 1989 that plans were announced for a monument to the men and women who had served in the Korean War.

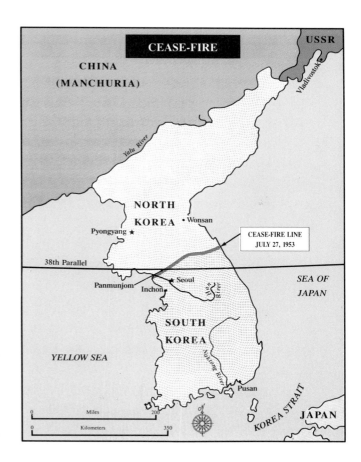

Between 1950 and 1953, the North Koreans and Chinese captured 7,140 Americans for certain. (Many of the Americans listed as missing in action may have been captured and murdered, but how many isn't known.) Of these, 2,701 Americans died in captivity—a shocking 38 percent. Conditions in the Communist POW camps were terrible for most of the war. Prisoners had little food, unclean water, few blankets, and almost no medical care.

The Korean War was also a conflict in which one side—the Communists—tried to convert prisoners to its beliefs.

The term *brainwashing* comes from the Chinese phrase for "thought reform." This was a program developed by the Chinese in 1946. The Chinese had used thought reform to convert captured Nationalist Chinese soldiers to the Communist cause.

In order to brainwash POWs, prisoners were kept alone in small cells for long periods with little or no sleep. Their captors talked to them constantly about what was "wrong" with their country. The captors continually pointed out the supposed benefits of communism. Finally, the Communists offered relief, in the form of food and sleep, if POWs confessed "past crimes and errors of belief."

Over time, some prisoners gave in. Many "confessed" because they felt it wouldn't hurt anyone and would make their lives easier. But a few POWs, about 15 percent, did help their captors to an extent the army called "serious collaboration." In one case, an American air force crew was brainwashed and tortured into confessing to U.S. use of germ warfare. The Communists used this charge, later proved untrue, in much of their propaganda.

When POWs from both sides were exchanged before the armistice, twenty-one American soldiers and one British marine decided to stay in Communist China rather than come home. This shocked many Americans and Britons. Also troubling was the fact that some prisoners agreed to act as Communist agents on their return home.

After a study of POW behavior, the army realized that many of the "collaborators" gave in because they were unprepared for the rigors of captivity. To prevent this from happening in future wars, the army drew up a Code of Conduct for its soldiers. The code clearly outlined the responsibility of POWs to their country and fellow prisoners. The military also began training soldiers, marines, and air personnel in SERE (Survival, Escape, Resistance, and Evasion) techniques to better survive, or escape from, captivity.

These programs must be called successful, because the behavior of Americans captured in Vietnam was much better than that of American prisoners taken in Korea.

THE PRISONERS

Life magazine photographer Hank Walker took this picture of terrified Chinese soldiers, flushed from their hiding place by U.S. infantrymen, wordlessly asking for mercy. They were taken prisoner but in the heat of battle some units did not "take prisoners."

© 1951 LIFE PICTURE SERVICE

This previously unpublished photo, provided by Kang Nak Rhee, director of the ROK National Police, is captioned "Evidence of Communist savagery—families of ROK armed forces and police were slaughtered at 1500 hours, October 15, 1950."

LIBRARY OF CONGRESS

Some of the twenty-two Americans who, with a single British marine, decided not to return home after the conflict. Over 22,000 North Koreans and Chinese also elected not to go back to their Communist homelands.

WIDE WORLD

AFTERWORD

A SOMETIMES VIOLENT PEACE

The armistice agreement did not "win" the war, since neither North Korea nor the UN had made a formal declaration of war. Also, the cease-fire did not stop all the shooting.

To separate the UN and Communist forces, the truce agreement established a "demilitarized zone," or DMZ. It exists to the present day. About two and a half miles wide, it runs 150 miles from the Yellow Sea to the Sea of Japan along the 38th parallel. It is heavily fortified on both sides: thousands of American and South Korean servicemen and -women are stationed along the DMZ.

Meetings at the truce village of Panmunjom continue regularly. Sometimes the North Koreans walk out, as they did often during the original talks. Shooting incidents between North Koreans and

Olympic Park in Seoul was the site of the highly successful 1988 Summer Olympic Games. Despite threats of terrorism from North Korea, more nations participated in the games than ever before.

members of the UN command still happen occasionally. Fifty-eight Americans and over 300 South Koreans died in sniper attacks and ambushes between the 1953 cease-fire and 1982.

Two serious incidents took place in 1968. On January 22, in the Sea of Japan off the North Korean coast, North Korean torpedo boats surrounded the small U.S. Navy intelligence (spy) ship *Pueblo.* The *Pueblo* carried sophisticated electronic gear to monitor North Korean military activity. The North Koreans brought the *Pueblo* into the port of Wonsan, even though the ship had been cruising in international waters. The *Pueblo's* crew of eighty-three men was imprisoned in harsh conditions for nearly a year. The United States uses such ships to keep track of North Korean movements so another surprise attack won't occur.

In the same week of the *Pueblo's* capture, thirty-one North Korean terrorists slipped across the DMZ. They almost succeeded in attacking the Blue House,

57

Hundreds of violent episodes have occurred in the DMZ separating the two Koreas. Here, a U.S. officer is murdered with an ax by North Korean soldiers.

the South Korean presidential palace. South Korean police stopped them in a bloody shoot-out. A surviving terrorist said the team's mission had been to behead ROK President Park Chung Hee and throw his head in the street. "We were told," he said, "that by eliminating Park, we would bring chaos to South Korea and inspire fear. We could stop the progress South Korea is making."

The Republic of Korea has made dramatic progress in rebuilding a land and economy shattered by the war. The entire peninsula had been wrecked by the conflict. At the war's end, in one historian's words, "Both North and South Korea were devastated. Bridges were down, rail lines broken, tunnels blocked, ports filled with junk, buildings gutted, irrigation and hydroelectric

systems ruined. The countryside was barren."

But from the wreckage of 1953, South Korea has risen to become one of the fastest-growing industrial nations. The country's booming factories produce cars, computers, appliances, and many other products. South Korea has become a major economic power not only in Asia but in the world. Only Japan, the United States, and West Germany produce and sell more computer memory chips than South Korea. This spectacular growth has changed South Korea from a rural society to an industrial one in only a few years. In 1965, more than half of South Korea's workers were farmers. Today, fewer than one-quarter are farmers. And South Korea's per capita income (the average yearly income per person) tripled in just two decades, from 1961 to 1980.

Despite this economic recovery, political progress toward traditional democracy has come slowly. President Syngman Rhee resigned in 1960 after an election fraud scandal. Rhee's successor, General Park Chung Hee, gained power in a military takeover. He imprisoned opponents, declared martial law (rule by the military) in 1975, and in 1978 rigged elections to stay in power. Park was then assassinated in 1979 by the director of the ROK Central Intelligence Agency. After the assassination, another general, Chun Doo Hwan, took over the government. Chun ruled South Korea with an iron hand, imprisoning over 10,000 political opponents, including Kim Dae Jung, a prominent spokesman for democracy. Kim is now head of a political party and a member of the National Assembly, South Korea's lawmaking body.

In 1985, Chun's party managed to hold on to a majority in the National Assembly, but opposition was growing. In 1987, after a year of violent protests by students and labor activists, President Chun surprised the world. He agreed to adopt a new constitution, guaranteeing freedom of the press, more political power for the national assembly, and shorter presidential terms.

In 1988, Seoul, by then the world's fifth-largest city, was the site of the Summer Olympics. The games gave South Korea a chance to show off its miracle economy. Although North Korea threatened to disrupt the games,

In April 1960, student uprisings toppled the Syngman Rhee government. Unrest continues among students unhappy with South Korea's strict central government.

only Cuba and Nicaragua refused to participate. One hundred sixty-one nations sent athletes to the Seoul Olympics, twenty-one more than ever before. In the same year, South Korea held its first direct presidential election in sixteen years. Chun was succeeded by Roh Tae Woo.

The struggle for full democracy in South Korea continues. In the 1988 National Assembly elections, the opposition parties gained a majority over President Roh's party. However, several political dissidents were jailed in 1989.

One reason South Korea's leaders have forcefully silenced their opponents is the continuing tension with North Korea. The North Koreans continue to use assassination and other terrorist actions to undermine South Korea's government.

A young Korean in traditional dress at the United Nations cemetery in Pusan.

Exact figures on the damage the war caused to North Korea are unavailable. However, it is clear that North Korea suffered even more destruction than South Korea. But today, while South Korea's economy is going strong, North Korea's economy has experienced difficulties. Kim Il Sung continues to head North Korea's Communist government. In 1980, he named his son, Kim Jong Il, head of the North Korean Communist Party. This put him in line for his father's job as dictator.

North Korea remains greatly isolated from the world at large. In 1977, the country defaulted (failed to pay monies due) on some $2 billion in international loans. Many nations have cut off further loans. Later, world opinion was outraged when North Korean terrorists bombed a meeting in Rangoon, Burma, in 1983. They killed seventeen people, including four South Korean cabinet members. In 1987, in an effort to disrupt the Olympics, North Korean terrorists placed a bomb aboard a Korean Airlines airliner, which blew up near Burma, killing 115 people.

The relations between the two Koreas improved somewhat in 1984. In that year, severe floods hit South Korea. North Korea sent food and building materials south in a humanitarian gesture. Since 1971, the governments of North and

In 1989, President George Bush announced plans for a Korean War Veterans Monument to be built in Washington. This is an architect's rendering of the proposed monument.

South Korea have met under the sponsorship of the International Red Cross to discuss the possible reunification of the two nations into a single Korea. No major progress has been made. But in 1985, civilians and performing artists from both North and South Korea were allowed to cross the DMZ to visit relatives and perform.

The Korean War was a bloody part of a larger conflict—the cold war. Today, however, many people believe the cold war is ending, or at least subsiding. Some Communist nations remain fiercely competitive with the free world. They continue to practice terrorism and repression of their own people to hold and expand their power. Yet by 1990 some countries moved dramatically toward democracy, even to the point of arresting or executing their dictators.

But the Soviet Union and China in particular appear to be realizing that they cannot build healthy economies without dealing peacefully with the rest of the world. Someday, perhaps, North Korea will follow the example of its former allies. In the meantime, however, thousands of American troops continue to keep watch in the Land of the Morning Calm.

INDEX

Page numbers in *italics* indicate illustrations.

RESOURCE GUIDE

Suggested Reading

Hastings, Max. *The Korean War*. New York: Simon & Schuster, 1987.

Knox, Donald. *The Korean War: Pusan to Chosin*. New York: Harcourt Brace Jovanovich, 1985.

————. *The Korean War: Uncertain Victory*. New York: Harcourt Brace Jovanovich, 1987.

Korea Overseas Information Service. *A Handbook of Korea*. Seoul International Publishing House, 1988.

Weisberger, Bernard. *Cold War, Cold Peace*. New York: American Heritage, 1984.

Suggested Viewing

M.A.S.H. (TCF/Aspen, 1970)

Pork Chop Hill (United Artists, 1959)

The Bridges at Toko-Ri (Paramount, 1954)

The Manchurian Candidate (United Artists, 1962)